LARGE PRINT
BUTTERFLIES
COLORING BOOK

LARGE PRINT
BUTTERFLIES
COLORING BOOK

SIRIUS

SIRIUS

This edition published in 2024 by Sirius Publishing, a division of
Arcturus Publishing Limited,
26/27 Bickels Yard, 151–153 Bermondsey Street,
London SE1 3HA

Copyright © Arcturus Holdings Limited

ISBN: 978-1-3988-4490-2
CH012194NT

Printed in China

Introduction

Coloring has been shown to be an excellent and creative way for both children and adults to relieve stress as well as improving concentration and manual dexterity. Often, as you get older your eyesight becomes less acute and discerning small and elaborate designs may be difficult. For this reason, the images in this book have been chosen specifically for their bold, clear outlines, simplicity, and lack of visual "clutter."

There are many butter-flies to choose from, some graphic and rendered as patterns, others more real-istic. Some are captured fluttering in movement or in groups, while others are solitary and still.

To get yourself in the mood, find somewhere away from your every-day tasks—and especially from work. Choose either colored pencils or markers if you prefer, select a design you like, and take a couple of hours to color your own special butterfly illustration.

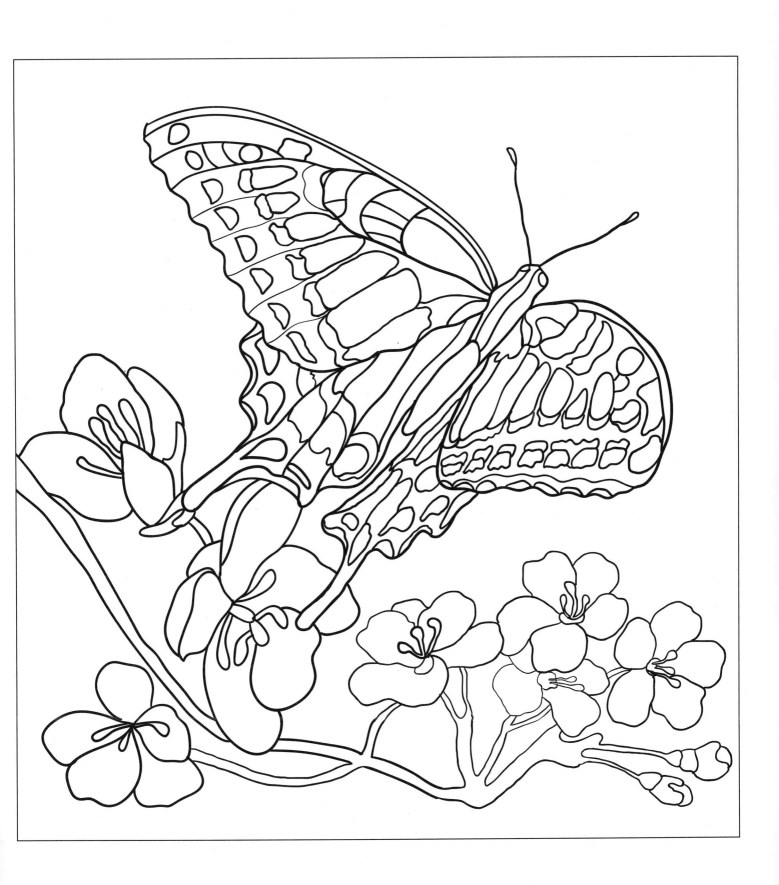